YOSEMITE

NATIONAL PARK

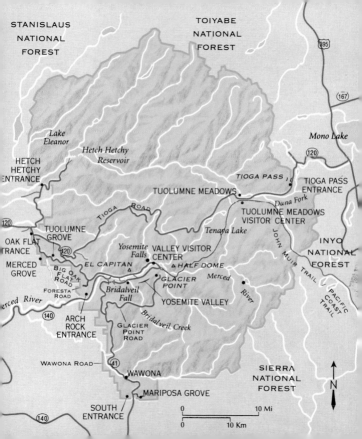

YOSEMITE
NATIONAL PARK

NATIONAL PARKS AND
CONSERVATION ASSOCIATION

———

by David Dunbar
Photography by Jerry Pavia

A TINY FOLIO™
Abbeville Press · Publishers
New York · London · Paris

FRONT COVER: Half Dome
BACK COVER: A seasonal waterfall near Tunnel View on Wawona Road
SPINE: California poppies
PAGE 4: Arch Rock on El Portal Road

EDITOR: Susan Costello
DESIGNER: Celia Fuller
PRODUCTION EDITOR: Meredith Wolf
PRODUCTION MANAGER: Lou Bilka
MAPS: Guenter Vollath

FIRST EDITION
2 4 6 8 10 9 7 5 3 1

Library of Congress Cataloging-in-Publication Data
Dunbar, David.
Yosemite National Park / by David Dunbar; photography by Jerry Pavia.
p. cm.
"National Parks and Conservation Association"
"A tiny folio"
Includes bibliographical references and index.
ISBN 0-7892-0106-2
1. Yosemite National Park (Calif.) 2. Yosemite National Park (Calif.)—Pictorial works. I. Pavia, Jerry II. National Parks and Conservation Association. III. Title.
F868.Y6D86 1996
979.4′47—dc20   95-45352
CIP

CONTENTS

PREFACE

When Yosemite National Park came into being, America had just begun to realize that its spectacular wilderness could be vulnerable to exploitation.

Indeed, Yosemite may have first inspired the concept of national parks. In 1833, long before the National Park System was created, naturalist George Catlin wrote that Yosemite could be "a Nation's park containing man and beast, in all the wild and freshness of their nature's beauty." First explored by Native Americans, and later by trappers, miners, and pioneers, Yosemite and its wonders were chronicled by J. M. Hutchings and other writers in the late 1850s. Horace Greeley visited Yosemite in 1859 and wrote, "I know no single wonder of Nature on earth which can claim a superiority over the Yosemite."

Soon Frederick Law Olmsted was dispatched to this incredible place in the midst of his efforts to establish Central Park in New York City. Olmsted and others encouraged President Lincoln to preserve Yosemite, and on June 30, 1864, at the height of the Civil War, Yosemite Valley was granted to California as a public trust.

Probably more American leaders have fought for the preservation of Yosemite than any other park. John Muir struggled for years to protect Yosemite and the surrounding valleys from exploitation, and his writings helped bring about its establishment as a national park. Named a World Heritage Site in 1985, Yosemite serves as a model for other scenic wonders that are now part of the National Park System.

Today, Yosemite continues to stand as a symbol of the conflict about whether or not to preserve our natural heritage. While some seek to capture the wealth that comes from millions of visitors every year, others fight to save the air and water from pollution and to preserve some measure of solitude and sanctity.

We must decide whether Yosemite and other national parks will continue to be battlegrounds for humanity's diverse and conflicting expectations of nature, or places that offer people respite in difficult times. That is the challenge of our age.

PAUL C. PRITCHARD
President, National Parks and Conservation Association

INTRODUCTION

Considered by many to be the scenic crown jewel of American national parks, Yosemite lies at the midpoint of the Sierra Nevada, the mountains that pioneering conservationist and naturalist John Muir called the "Range of Light." More than 90 percent of this vast preserve is wilderness, an unspoiled high-country realm of evergreen forests, flowered meadows, ponds and lakes, deep canyons, snowy summits, barren granite ridges and domes, and, above all, solitude.

The Yosemite most familiar to nature lovers around the world is a small U-shaped valley in the southwestern section of the park; Muir called it the "Incomparable Valley." Many of the millions who come to the park each

OPPOSITE. Mariposa Grove's giant sequoias, the world's largest living things.

year see it and little else in a preserve the size of Rhode Island. A granite-walled corridor just a mile (1.6 km) wide and seven miles (11.2 km) long, Yosemite Valley is one of the most recognizable landscapes on earth, a remarkably dense concentration of scenic wonders.

Guarding the entrance to this hallowed gorge is El Capitan (Spanish for "The Chief"), a sheer cliff that juts into the valley like the prow of an immense ocean liner. It is the world's largest exposed granite monolith—twice the height of the Rock of Gibraltar. Opposite El Capitan, on the southern wall of the canyon, gossamer Bridalveil Fall spills over the lip of a hanging valley, often turning into a windblown filmy mist before it reaches an alcove 620 feet (189 m) below.

Both sides of the valley compete for attention in a procession of mountain majesty. Jagged incisors called the Cathedral Rocks buttress the canyon walls on the south. Across the valley on the north thunders the two-part symphony of wind-whipped spray that is Yosemite Fall. Back on the south side loom Sentinel Dome, a bald granite globe, and Glacier Point atop a towering rampart. Opposite, the Royal Arches stack convex ribs on a sloping granite wall. The eastern end of the valley is dominated by the mysterious cowled hulk of Half

Dome, which Muir called "the most beautiful and most sublime of all the wonderful Yosemite rocks."

Unlike the Rockies, the central section of the Sierra Nevada is not a chain of individual mountains. Instead, it is a massive block of granite some 400 miles (645 km) long and up to 80 miles (130 km) wide. The granite was formed from molten rock at the roots of a chain of volcanoes much like today's Cascade Range. This subterranean mass, known as a batholith, formed 200 million to 80 million years ago.

During the past 25 million years, sedimentary and volcanic rock overlying this granitic mass weathered and eroded away. Then, about 10 million years ago, the whole region underwent a tremendous but uneven uplift that tilted the landscape southwestward. The accelerated flow of the Merced, Tuolumne, and other rivers carved ever-deeper valleys in the stubborn rock.

Geologic uplift also played a major role in creating Yosemite's cliffs and domes. Bedrock cracks—called joints—formed as the uplifted granite cooled and was exposed by erosion. When these joints are vertical, the rock flakes off over the eons into massive cliffs, such as El Capitan.

When the joints are flat or convex, they form great

round domes nearly devoid of vegetation. As temperatures change, the granite expands and contracts; this causes horizontal cracks to form and layers to develop in the rock. Gradually the granite's top layer rises, breaks apart, and peels off like an onion shedding its skins. This exfoliation relieves the pressure on the layer beneath, giving it room to rise. Granite is the only rock that forms these relatively rare formations; Yosemite has the world's largest collection.

By 3 million years ago, the central Sierra was nearly at its present elevation. Then the eastern scarp of the range rose another 3,000 feet (915 m), creating the Sierra's impressive eastern crest and tilting the landscape even more. Rushing mountain rivers turned into torrents that sliced downward through the rock in steep, V-shaped canyons.

In the last 2 million years great rivers of ice put the finishing touches on Yosemite's present appearance. The final uplift of the eastern Sierra thrust summits into thin, cold air; snowpacks lingering year-round on protected slopes eventually turned into glaciers. When continental ice sheets advanced over much of Canada and the northeastern and midwestern United States, glaciers inched down from the Sierran crest, creating local ice fields as much as a mile (1.6 km) thick

These alpine glaciers gnawed rounded Sierra summits into angular, hollow-sided peaks and whittled knife-edged ridges called arêtes. Ice quarried and carried away great blocks from rough canyon walls to fashion sheer cliffs. Outlet glaciers flowing from the ice fields down preexisting river valleys turned the water-carved, V-shaped corridors into the park's spectacular U-shaped troughs.

As advancing glaciers excavated the valley of the Merced River, tributary glaciers along Yosemite Creek, Bridalveil Creek, and other secondary waterways cut much more slowly. Their valleys were eventually left hanging high above the ever-deepening valley of the Merced. When the ice retreated some 10,000 years ago, streams in these hanging valleys had to leap over high cliffs to reach the Merced far below.

The classic example of a hanging-valley waterfall is Yosemite Fall, at 2,425 feet (739 m) the highest waterfall in North America. Another type of Yosemite waterfall is the "glacial stairway" that results from the action of glaciers plucking huge blocks out of streambeds along granite joints. In Little Yosemite Valley, the Merced River drops 2,000 feet (610 m) in 1.5 miles (2.4 km) as

1 WAWONA REGION

2 YOSEMITE VALLEY REGION

3 TIOGA ROAD REGION

it tumbles through a maelstrom called the Giant's Stairway; 594-foot (181-m) Nevada Fall and 317-foot (96-m) Vernal Fall spill over two of its steps.

In a landscape filled with perpendiculars, it's not surprising that the park's most impressive flora should be a tree that soars more than 300 feet (90 m) from forest floor to crown. Three groves of giant sequoias, the world's largest living things, dot western Yosemite: the Mariposa Grove near the park's southern boundary, and the Merced and Tuolumne groves west of Yosemite Valley.

With their decay-resistant wood protected from insects, disease, and all but the most intense conflagrations by bark two feet (.6 m) thick, these "vegetable Titans" (in the words of nineteenth-century Boston preacher Thomas Starr King) live as long as 3,000 years—a lifespan surpassed only by the bristlecone pine, some of which are more than 4,000 years old. The oldest sequoia known today is a 2,700-year-old behemoth in the Mariposa Grove known as the Grizzly Giant.

A welcome change from this relentless verticality is provided by the High Sierra's alpine meadows. Largest of all is Tuolumne, an open, grassy basin sliced by the Tuolumne River and surrounded by peaks. From June to mid-August, shooting star, fireweed, aster, penste-mon, mountain pride, and other wildflowers soften the stark beauty of the high country.

The earliest evidence of humankind in what is now the park dates from around 1400 B.C., mainly pic-tographs and crude stone implements. Around 1200 A.D. these ancient peoples were replaced by ancestors of the southern Miwoks, who called their new home *Ahwahnee*, "the Place of the Big Mouth," referring to the entrance of Yosemite Valley, and called themselves Ahwahneechee.

The Ahwahneechee built dwellings, assembly houses, and sweat lodges from the woven branches of deer-brush, grapevine, and conifer and cedar-bark shingles. Abundant black oak acorns were a staple of the Ahwah-neechee diet. Women collected the acorns and stored them in free-standing granaries. Each family consumed about 500 pounds (230 kg) of acorns a year, all painstakingly shelled, pounded into a fine flour, leached repeatedly to remove bitter tannic acid, and cooked into soup, mush, and cakes.

The first explorers to see Yosemite country were prob-ably frontiersman Joseph Walker and his fur trappers in 1833. For two decades Ahwahnee remained a forgotten mountain valley. Then gold was discovered in California, and prospectors flooded the Sierra foothills, clashing with local tribes who saw their land being overrun.

Most California tribes accepted treaties; not the Ahwahneechees, whom other Miwoks called *yo'hem-iteh,* which was corrupted into "Yosemetos" and "Yosemites." In 1851 a volunteer militia, the "Mariposa Battalion," was dispatched to secure the surrender of the Yosemites. The soldiers followed a route similar to today's Wawona Road to the valley.

The expedition was a failure: under an aged chief named Tenaya, the Indians easily eluded the battalion. Nevertheless, within two years the Awahneechees were forced out of their mountain homeland and onto a reservation on the Fresno River. Two years after that, in 1855, the first tourist party arrived, eager to see the radiantly beautiful valley that had awed the Mariposa soldiers. The nation's early conservationists campaigned to protect not only the valley but also a grove of giant sequoias from a rush of homesteaders and hotelkeepers.

On June 30, 1864, with the Civil War raging, President Lincoln signed a bill entrusting both the valley and the Mariposa Grove to California, requiring the

Muir's "crystal Merced" flows past the distant Cathedral Rocks and other promontories lining Yosemite Valley.

state to preserve and protect "the premises" in a natural, undisturbed condition. The Yosemite Grant created America's first state park. It was also the first time that the United States (or any nation) had sought to preserve wilderness.

Largely through the efforts of John Muir, the Sierra Club's first president, Yosemite became a national park in 1890, although it was not until 1906 that California formally gave the original grants back to the federal government. More land was added in 1913, the year automobiles were first allowed in Yosemite.

"This one noble park is big enough and rich enough for a whole life of study and aesthetic enjoyment," wrote Muir. "Its natural beauty cleanses and warms like fire, and you will be willing to stay forever in one place like a tree."

One of America's best-loved national parks protects a treasury of Sierra Nevada beauty. Here in east-central California snowy granite summits rise majestically, bare domes of granite bulge above the landscape, deep winter snows feed springtime torrents that spill over cliffs as some of the world's highest waterfalls, and ancient trees soar like skyscrapers.

22   As shown on the map on pages 16-17, Yosemite may

be divided into three touring regions based on the park's 450 miles (725 km) of highways. The Wawona Region (1) in the southwest corner of Yosemite takes in the Mariposa Grove of giant sequoias, the historic settlement of Wawona, and the Glacier Point Road to a scenic belvedere.

The park's centerpiece is the Yosemite Valley Region (2). Spectacular scenery and quiet beauty fill this narrow mountain corridor in the southwestern part of Yosemite: cliffs and other mesmerizing granite formations, thundering waterfalls, and soothing forests of oak, pine, fir, and cedar alongside the winding Merced River.

The Tioga Road Region (3) provides access to the park's hinterlands, the forested realm of mule deer, black bears, and elusive wildcats. Tioga Road, which cuts across the center of Yosemite, passes stupendous viewpoints, compelling geological formations, and High Sierra meadows, then scales the highest road pass in California.

SCENIC TOURS

The following portfolios portray the scenic magnificence of Yosemite. The photographs are organized into three touring regions, each accompanied by a map that shows roads and service areas and pinpoints natural wonders, scenic lookouts, and other places of interest.

The Wawona Region (Tour 1) embraces the southwest quadrant of the park. A cathedral hush stills Mariposa Grove, largest in Yosemite, with 500 mature trees. It's difficult to believe that these cinnamon-colored columns with elephantine bases are living things that grew from a seed the size of an oatmeal flake. The largest, although not the tallest, tree is the Grizzly Giant. Its base is thirty feet (9 m) in diameter; a huge

---

A grove of California black oaks in Yosemite Valley frames
El Capitan, the world's largest solid granite block.

limb halfway up the trunk is thought to be larger than any tree east of the Mississippi.

Galen Clark, the "Guardian of Yosemite," began homesteading at nearby Wawona Meadows in 1856. Three brothers from Vermont named Washburn made the area a stagecoach stop on their toll road to Yosemite Valley (in the 1850s a round-trip on their bone-rattling turnpike cost a man and a horse $2). Visitors still rusticate at the Washburn's Wawona Hotel, the oldest resort hotel in California (1879). In summer a stagecoach takes visitors from the hotel across the South Fork of the Merced on the brothers' New England–style covered bridge to tour the Pioneer Yosemite History Center.

Farther north, Glacier Point Road leads to Yosemite's most impressive lookout, a rocky ledge more than 3,000 feet (915 m) above Yosemite Valley. All around are the park's star attractions: Half Dome, Sentinel Dome, Vernal and Nevada falls, and the high country.

A final scenic stunner awaits back on the Wawona Road at the end of a long tunnel. The Tunnel View Overlook may be the most photographed vista on earth, embracing the waterfalls and colossal rocks of Yosemite Valley.

Tour 2, the Yosemite Valley Region, approaches the park from the west on Highway 140 (El Portal Road). Completed in 1926 by convict labor, the road ascends the canyon of the lower Merced River, a rugged, V shaped gorge never touched by Pleistocene glaciers. This stretch of the Merced River is probably what Yosemite Valley looked like before the Ice Age.

The highway passes beneath Arch Rock, two huge boulders that form a natural portal, then angles northeast on the north bank of the rushing Merced River. Past Wildcat Falls, the waters of Cascade and Tamarack creeks surge over individual cataracts, then merge on the sloping canyon wall before plunging together 500 feet (152 m) in a combined hydraulic plume called The Cascades.

Continuing upstream, the highway skirts roiling, boulder-choked rapids, then abruptly encounters flat water, which signals entry into the heart of the park. Wild Merced Canyon widens into gentle Yosemite Valley, a mosaic of grassy meadows, pleasant oak woodlands, and mixed-conifer forests. Lining this flat-bottomed corridor are cliffs tasseled with waterfalls, angular monoliths, domes, pinnacles, and other commanding battlements.

In addition to these natural marvels, the valley tour also showcases human involvement in the park, from Paiute and Miwok baskets in the Indian Cultural Exhibit to the starkly beautiful photographs in the Ansel Adams Gallery. Valley structures range from a sacred Ahwahneechee sweat lodge to the gracious Ahwahnee Hotel.

Tour 3, the Tioga Road Region, centers around the highway that crosses the midsection of the park, climbing forty-six miles (74 km) from the foothills into the glorious alpine world. North of the blacktop lies the last wilderness in the High Sierra.

About ten miles (16 km) along Tioga Road, just beyond the turnoff for White Wolf Lodge, the forest parts to reveal views toward snowy peaks along the Sierran crest. Four miles (6.4 km) farther east a road-cut through the side of a dome graphically displays how the granite arches upward in thick slabs. The Clouds Rest Viewpoint is a High Sierra panorama of knobbly granite summits and deep gorges.

The most impressive stop is Olmsted Point, with its views of Tenaya Canyon's deep slash into the bedrock, Clouds Rest, the hunched shoulders of Half Dome, and Tenaya Lake lapping the base of glacier-polished mountains and ridges. The Indians' more descriptive name for this body of water was *Pywiack,* "Lake of Shining Rocks."

Centerpiece of the drive is Tuolumne Meadows, the largest subalpine meadow in the Sierra Nevada. This lawnlike expanse erupts in early July with a Technicolor wildflower explosion that lasts until August. The route ends at the narrow cleft of Tioga Pass, elevation 9,945 feet (3,031 m).

TOUR 1 WAWONA REGION

This drive totals sixty-eight miles (109 km); budget a half to a full day. Take Highway 41 (Wawona Road) to the South Entrance, then turn right at a T junction and drive two miles (3.2 km) southeast to Mariposa Grove. Arrive early; in summer parking lots sometimes fill by 10:00 A.M., and park officials close the road. Trails through the Lower and Upper groves begin at the parking lot.

Return to the T junction, then continue five miles (8 km) north on Highway 41 to Wawona, the site of a historic hotel, a golf course, riding stables, and other visitor facilities.

Twelve miles (19 km) north of Wawona, turn right onto Glacier Point Road. The Taft Point and Sentinel Dome hikes start at the parking lot on the left 13.5 miles (21.7 km) from the Wawona-Glacier Point junction. Glacier Point Road ends 2.5 miles (4 km) farther north. Spectacular views of Yosemite Valley are just a short walk from the parking lot.

Backtrack to Highway 41, then go fifteen miles (24 km) north. Just after exiting the Wawona Tunnel, pull into the Tunnel View Overlook for more awe-inspiring valley vistas. The highway then winds down to the Merced River.

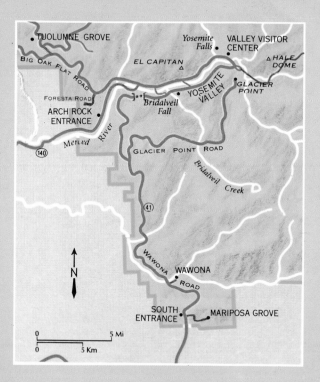

TUOLUMNE GROVE

BIG OAK FLAT ROAD

FORESTA ROAD

ARCH ROCK
ENTRANCE

Merced River

(140)

*Yosemite
Falls*

EL CAPITAN

*Bridalveil
Fall*

YOSEMITE
VALLEY

VALLEY VISITOR
CENTER

△ HALF
DOME

GLACIER
POINT

GLACIER POINT ROAD

Bridalveil Creek

(41)

N

WAWONA

ROAD

WAWONA

SOUTH
ENTRANCE

MARIPOSA GROVE

0   5 Mi
0   5 Km

ABOVE. At 96 feet (9 m) in diameter and 209 feet (19 m) in height, the Grizzly Giant is the largest sequoia in the Mariposa Grove, as well as the oldest known sequoia (2,700 years) in the world.
OPPOSITE. More than 500 giant sequoias grow in Mariposa's Upper and Lower Groves.

Wawona Meadows, a verdant expanse along the South Fork
of the Merced River.

Miniature lupines and other wildflowers spike a grassy
Wawona meadow.

Sentinel Dome, accessible from Glacier Point Road.

Sentinel Dome, more than 4,000 feet (1219 m) above the
floor of Yosemite Valley.

Whitebark pine along a ridge on Sentinel Dome.

Half Dome at sunrise from Sentinel Dome.

Above. Dawn's early light gleams on El Capitan's brow,
as seen from Sentinel Dome.
Opposite. Strong winds spray the waters of Upper Yosemite
Fall into a tassel of spray and mist.

ABOVE. Dead but still standing, a Jeffrey pine as bleached
as driftwood clings tenaciously to the obdurate crown
of Sentinel Dome.

OPPOSITE. Looking northeast across Yosemite Valley
from Sentinel Dome at dusk, North Dome and
smaller Basket Dome rise round and barren from
cliffs framing Tenaya Canyon.

ABOVE. Half Dome at dusk from Sentinel Dome.
PAGES 44–45. The eastern crest of the Sierra Nevada forms a
formidable and wintry backdrop to Yosemite's high
country, as seen at sundown from Sentinel Dome.

46

Half Dome, a cracked granite block that rises 4,733 feet (1442 m).

ABOVE. At the Fissures near Taft Point, small boulders jam in the narrowing walls of deep, narrow clefts.
OPPOSITE. Yosemite granite parts wide enough in one of the Fissures to reveal the southern wall of Yosemite Valley.

49

ABOVE. Evergreens crown a ridge at Taft Point.
OPPOSITE. Taft Point, an overhanging promontory of
cracked and jumbled granite, caps Yosemite Valley's sheer,
3,000-foot (914-m) southern rim.

Above. Taft Point in the foreground, El Capitan
in the distance.
Opposite. Yosemite Fall from Taft Point.

Pages 54–55. In Little Yosemite Valley, the Merced River spills over 594-foot (181-m) Nevada Fall, foams a short distance over a boulder-strewn bed, then drops another 319 feet (97 m) as Vernal Fall before easing into flat-bottomed Yosemite Valley.

North Dome (left), Half Dome, and Vernal Fall from
Washburn Point.

North Dome (left) and Basket Dome from Washburn Point.

Above. From Glacier Point the hulking presence of
Half Dome, shown here at sunset, dominates a view
crowded with Yosemite's scenic wonders.
Opposite. Half Dome's upper 700 feet (213 m) remained
uncovered even at the height of Pleistocene glaciation.

North Dome from Glacier Point.

High Sierra, the wilderness heart of the park, as seen from
Glacier Point.

ABOVE. A seasonal waterfall rushes through a wooded
glen near Tunnel View on Wawona Road.
OPPOSITE. Bridalveil Fall spills over the lip of a textbook
example of a hanging valley.

PAGES 64–65. El Capitan at dusk, seen from Tunnel View.

TOUR 2 YOSEMITE VALLEY REGION

Totalling just twenty miles (32 km), this tour can be driven in a few hours, but the valley is filled with so many points of interest that most travelers fill an entire day or two with stops and nature walks.

The tour begins at the Arch Rock Entrance on Highway 140 (El Portal Road). Three miles (5 km) northeast are Cascade Falls. Another 1.6 miles (2.5 km) brings you to the junction of Highway 140 and Highway 120 (Big Oak Flat Road). Another .8 miles (1.2 km) east on Highway 140, bear right and cross Pohono Bridge to the south bank of the Merced. In the next seven miles (11.2 km) the one-way road passes Bridalveil Fall, Cathedral Rock, and Cathedral Spires en route to Curry Village at the base of Glacier Point.

Roads up-valley from Curry Village are restricted to bicycles and shuttlebuses. Park your car at the day-use lot and walk .6 miles (1 km) or take the free shuttle southeast to the Happy Isles Nature Center, departure point for the trail to Vernal Fall, both on the Merced.

Back at Happy Isles, take the shuttlebus to the next stop, which provides access to the Mirror Lake trail. The shuttle stops again at Curry Village as it heads down-valley. Return to your car, cross the Merced, and take the westbound, one-way drive on the north bank of the river past Yosemite Village.

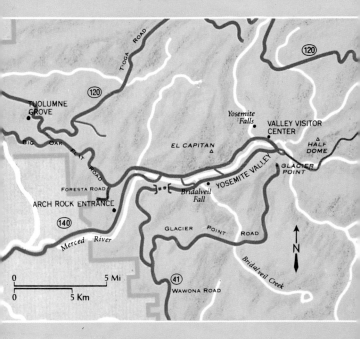

Next comes Yosemite Falls, where you can stroll from the parking lot to the base of the Lower Fall. Back on the drive, continue west past Yosemite Lodge and park at the Sunnyside Campground. From there, hikers can take the difficult switchback trail up the valley wall to scenic viewpoints of Upper Yosemite Fall.

The drive heads west past Rocky Point, El Capitan, and Pohono Bridge. At the junction of Highways 140 and 120, bear right on Highway 120. Drive three miles (4.8 km) and turn right on Foresta Road and park. Cross Big Oak Flat Road to reach the Big Oak Flat Trail opposite the entrance to Foresta Road.

Beyond Foresta Road, Big Oak Flat Road continues to gain elevation for the next six miles (9.6 km) as it heads west out of Yosemite Valley toward Crane Flat near Tuolumne Grove. Numerous turnouts along this stretch of road enable visitors to see the contrast between U-shaped Yosemite Valley and V-shaped Merced Canyon. The tour ends at the junction of Big Oak Flat Road and Tioga Road.

In summer as many as 20,000 people a day crowd into Yosemite Valley, producing almost urban traffic congestion. In the eastern end of the valley, consider touring on the shuttle, which links major hotels and sites. The best way to beat high-season traffic in the western end of the valley is to drive in the early morning when the light is magical.

A mule deer, the park's most abundant large mammal, browses along the nature trail.

Merced River rushing through the Merced Canyon west of
the Arch Rock Entrance.

Cascade Fall along El Portal Road.

Fern Spring, winter, Yosemite Valley.

Fern Spring, summer.

Above. Surging with snowmelt, Bridalveil Creek pearls over its bouldered bed.

Opposite. Bridalveil Creek spills 620 feet (189 m) in Bridalveil Fall, then rushes through a boulder-littered alcove before flowing into the Merced River.

Bridalveil Fall and the Leaning Tower, south wall of
Yosemite Valley.

ABOVE. Leaning Tower, a tilted granite pinnacle.
PAGES 78–79. The broad granite shoulders of El Capitan
guard the western entrance to Yosemite Valley.

Above. Eagle Peak, uppermost of the Three Brothers, is the highest point on the north rim of Yosemite Valley, 3,800 feet (1158 m) above the valley floor.
Opposite. Parallel fractures in granite produced the symmetry of the Three Brothers.

Merced River with Upper Yosemite Fall in the distance.

Nearly level floor of Yosemite Valley provides a flat-water respite for the Merced River before it tumbles through Merced Canyon.

Above. Sentinel Rock, named for its likeness to
a watchtower.
Opposite. After turning to mist and spray in its descent
from the Upper Fall, Yosemite Creek tumbles through a
narrow gorge stepped with six intermediate falls and rapids,
then flares into the Lower Fall.

Above. Below Glacier Point an "ephemeral" (intermittent) cascade called Staircase Falls spills from ledge to ledge for 1,300 feet (396 m).

Opposite. Heavy rains in spring and summer turn on the Royal Arch Cascade, which intermittently washes 1,250 feet (381 m) of the north wall of Yosemite Valley.

ABOVE. At 2,425 feet (739 m), Yosemite Fall is the fifth
highest waterfall in the world.
OPPOSITE. Glaciers fashioned the Royal Arches, graceful
granite shells decorating the north wall of Yosemite Valley.

89

Rock face, trail to Vernal Fall.

An oak fills the gap between two split rocks along the trail
to Vernal Fall.

Merced River foaming through Little Yosemite Valley.

Tumultuous waters of the Merced River below Vernal Fall.

Tenaya Creek spilling into Mirror Lake at the southwestern
end of Tenaya Canyon.

Mirror Lake, earning its name for clear reflections of Basket Dome (right) and North Dome.

Royal Arch Cascade flowing over the north wall of
Yosemite Valley.

Upper Yosemite Fall, at its thunderous best in spring and early summer.

Above. Half Dome rises above an evergreen screen.
Opposite. The Royal Arches and Half Dome stand at the
eastern end of Yosemite Valley.

The wintry Merced and Half Dome.

The rock shelf atop Half Dome is known as the Visor.

Shooting stars in Leidig Meadow, Yosemite Valley.

A meadow in Yosemite Valley, with Sentinel Rock
in the distance.

ABOVE. Yosemite Creek below the Lower Fall.
OPPOSITE. "This noble fall [Yosemite]," wrote Muir, "has [by] far the richest, as well as the most powerful, voice of all the falls of the Valley . . . The low bass, booming, reverberating tones, [is] heard under favorable circumstances five or six miles away. . . ."

Upper Yosemite Fall, a drop of 1,430 feet (435 m).

El Capitan from El Capitan Bridge over the Merced River.

ABOVE. Just before the Pohono Bridge a scenic viewpoint called Valley View, or Gates of the Valley, offers this imposing perspective of El Capitan.
OPPOSITE. Cathedral Rocks, like El Captain, is made of stronger, more erosion-resistant granite than the fractured, recessed rock of adjacent cliffs.

ABOVE. Cascade and Tamarack Creeks join to produce Cascade
Fall beyond the western entrance to Yosemite Valley.
PAGES 110–111. Bridalveil Fall, renowned for delicate rainbows
in its spray and mists, is humbled here by a grander arc in
summer rain.

El Capitan and Half Dome, the signature granite formations of Yosemite Valley.

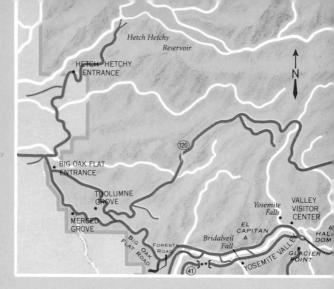

TOUR 3 TIOGA ROAD REGION

This tour is a scenic seventy-eight-mile (125-km) round-trip drive into the High Sierra through forests and past meadows, granite domes, lakes, and mountains. Budget a full day, with time set aside to stop at the numerous interpretive turnouts and to walk a short trail or two at Tuolumne Meadows.

Begin at the Big Oak Flat Entrance on Highway 120. At the junction of Big Oak Flat Road and Highway 120 (Tioga Road), bear right onto Tioga Road, which crosses the park

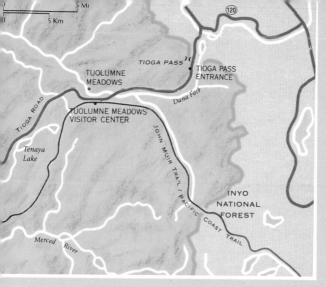

east–west. Just after the junction on the left is the parking lot for the Tuolumne Grove of giant sequoias.

Twenty-five miles (40.2 km) east, a short nature walk from the Olmsted Point parking lot crosses a glacier-scarred landscape. About seven miles (11.3 km) farther on is Tuolumne Meadows and its visitor center. About 1.5 miles (2.4 km) beyond the center is a parking lot on the left with a trail to Lembert Dome. The tour ends about ten miles (16 km) beyond the Meadows at Tioga Pass on the park's eastern boundary.

South fork of the Tuolumne River.

Tioga Road winds through extensive stands of red firs.

Mountain pride penstemon and Indian paintbrush soften
High Sierra granite.

Exfoliated granite along Tioga Road.

Twin western juniper snags.

Sloping, barren flanks of 9,926-foot (3025-m) Clouds Rest.

ABOVE. Mountain pride penstemon and an evergreen
seedling take root beneath a granite boulder.
OPPOSITE. Large, glacially transported boulders called erratics
litter the rockscape at Olmsted Point along Tioga Road.

The glacier-polished granite mountains that cup Tenaya Lake gave this High Sierra body of water its Indian name *Pywiack*—"Lake of the Shining Rocks."

Granite-rubbled ridge at Olmsted Point.

Western junipers live up to 2,000 years in Yosemite's wind-blasted highlands.

Rock-breaking roots of the western juniper at their
incremental work.

An unnamed High Sierra lakelet from Olmsted Point.

Western juniper clinging to a rock face below
Olmsted Point.

ABOVE. Early morning light warms an unnamed dome at
Tenaya Lake.
OPPOSITE. Mirrorlike waters of Tenaya Lake at sunrise.

Pywiack Dome, near Tenaya Lake along Tioga Road.

Silhouetted evergreens darken the foreground of a
gleaming, unnamed High Sierra dome at dusk. 133

Tuolumne Meadows, the Sierra Nevada's largest
subalpine meadow.

Tuolumne Meadows and distant Fairview Dome.

Above. The sharp spike of Unicorn Peak rises south of
Tuolumne Meadows.
Opposite. At an elevation of 8,600 feet (2621 m), Tuolumne
Meadows is a gateway to Yosemite's High Sierra.

Fairview Dome hems in Tuolumne Meadows on the south.

Unicorn Peak from Lembert Dome.

Above. The Dana Fork of the Tuolumne River joins the Lyell
Fork at Tuolumne Meadows.
Opposite. An unnamed lake backed by Mount Dana (left)
and Mount Gibbs, two mountains that form part of the
Sierra Nevada's soaring eastern crest.

Above. The High Sierra is dotted with seasonal ponds and lakelets after a winter of heavy snowfall.
Opposite. Mount Gibbs, a 12,764-foot (3890-m) summit straddling Yosemite's eastern boundary, forms a distant backdrop to the Dana Fork of the Tuolumne.

ABOVE. Sunning and eating: the yellow-bellied marmot's twin summer preoccupations.
OPPOSITE. Dana Fork of the Tuolumne near its source just north of 12,117-foot (3693-m) Mammoth Peak.

PAGES 146–147. The Dana Fork of the Tuolumne arises near the park's eastern boundary in a saddle between Mount Gibbs (right) and Mount Dana, at 13,053 feet (3979 m) the second highest summit in Yosemite.

WILDLIFE

Yosemite is famous for scenery, not for varied and vast animal populations. The mule deer, the park's most abundant large mammal, can be seen in the early morning or late afternoon browsing on mushrooms, berries, flowers, and grasses. If the deer senses danger it bounds away in a strange but speedy gait called a stott, a series of stiff-legged jumps in which all four feet hit the ground simultaneously.

Some 350 black bears, which can vary in color from light yellow through brown to black, roam Yosemite from valley bottoms to subalpine forests. These omnivores feed on grasses, berries, nuts, insects, rodents, and (rarely) the fawns of mule deer. Park bears, however,

---

A member of the park's healthy coyote population howls from a snowy bower.

often prefer the easier pickings around campsites.

Other Yosemite predators—coyotes, bobcats, gray foxes, mountain lions, fishers, eagles, and wolverines—are much more elusive. Small mammals such as squirrels, chipmunks, voles, moles, gophers, and shrews are seen more frequently.

High-country rock piles are home to the retiring pika and the sunbathing marmot, the park's largest member of the squirrel family. After a summer of grazing, an adult marmot weighs as much as seven pounds (3 kg). The Belding ground squirrel, a prairie dog lookalike, spends the brief alpine summer foraging in meadows, then hibernates eight months.

Bighorn sheep were eliminated early in the century after relentless hunting by miners and over-grazing of High Sierra meadows by domestic sheep. Reintroduced in 1986, bighorns now number about seventy in the eastern reaches of Yosemite.

The most prominent of Yosemite's 247 kinds of birds is the Steller's jay, a camp robber with beautiful blue plumage and a distinctive crest. American robins and band-tailed pigeons feast in September on the bright red berries of the Pacific dogwood. Red-winged blackbirds gather in autumn amid the willows and grasses of freshwater marshes along the lower Tuolumne and Merced rivers, then wing south.

In preparation for winter, the acorn woodpecker stores acorns harvested from California black oaks in holes it has bored into branches and trunks. This remarkable bird maneuvers the acorn's small end into the hole, then hammers with its beak until the acorn is flush with the tree. Squirrels and jays are usually unsuccessful at dislodging the woodpecker's cache.

Highland birds include the mountain bluebird, Clark's nutcracker, pine grosbeak, and gray-crowned rosy finch, which flits from one snowfield to another, eating insects that have been blown upward from lower elevations and immobilized by the cold. The dipper, sometimes called the ouzel, bobs alongside alpine streams, then dashes into the rushing waters, completely submerging itself to hunt for larvae on the bottom.

A pair of great gray owls.

The opossum, shown here in winter, remains sluggishly
active during cold weather.

The pallid bat lands near katydids, crickets, and other insect prey, then gives chase by crawling.

ABOVE. Golden-mantled ground squirrel hibernate from October to early spring.
OPPOSITE. Yellow-bellied marmots form colonies of a dominant male and a harem of two or three females and young.

Beaver lodge rises above a backcountry pond.

Once abundant beavers are now rare in Yosemite.

Young badgers peer through the grasses of a Yosemite meadow.

Ground squirrels are a staple of the badger's diet.

Ermine, or short-tailed weasel, wearing a winter coat
of white.

Like most weasels, the fisher remains active all winter,
ranging as much as three miles (4.8 km) a day in search of
rabbits, rodents, and other prey.

Long-tailed weasel inhabits the mixed-conifer forest in the upper montane zone up to about 8,000 feet (2438 m).

Partially webbed feet and thick, waterproof fur make the semiaquatic mink well-suited for hunting fish, frogs, and other prey in streams, lakes, and marshes.

ABOVE. Sleek, speedy river otters swim submerged to catch
trout and other freshwater fish.
OPPOSITE. Rare pine marten inhabits Yosemite's high-
elevation forests of mountain hemlocks and whitebark pines.

Slimmer than its striped cousin, the spotted skunk prefers
scrublands and other dry Yosemite habitats.

Striped skunks forage for rodents and other small mammals
in open mixed woods.

Rare in Yosemite (and elsewhere), the wolverine is a fearsome predator of high-elevation forests.

Coyote pounces on a rodent, then pins the prey with its paws.

ABOVE. Although the red fox is North America's most abundant and widespread fox species, it is rare in Yosemite. OPPOSITE. Primarily nocturnal gray fox, an excellent climber that can even jump from the branches of one tree to another. 171

Above. Looking for food or foe, a black bear rears up
on its hind legs amid a Yosemite meadow.
Opposite. Black bears, Yosemite's largest carnivores, range
throughout the park.

Unlike grizzlies, black bears are agile tree climbers, pushing off with their back legs and gripping with long-clawed forepaws.

Black bear cubs at play.

ABOVE. Mountain lion occasionally emerges during daylight
to sun itself on a ledge.
OPPOSITE. Nocturnal bobcat tracks its principal prey, the
mule deer, at dawn and dusk.

Mule deer, the park's most common large mammal, are most often seen in the Yosemite Valley and the Wawona Basin.

After an absence of 80 years, locally extirpated California bighorn sheep were reintroduced to the park in 1986.

Mallard drake at lift-off.

Harlequin duck flies fast and low over a swift mountain
stream, the preferred nesting site of the species.

Turkey vulture sunning on a snag.

Endangered bald eagle has a wingspan of up to
7½ feet (2.2 m).

ABOVE. Northern goshawk, a rare Yosemite species.
OPPOSITE. Northern harrier, which perches low and glides
just above the ground when hunting rodents, soars only
during acrobatic courtship displays.

Red-tailed hawks frequent Yosemite's foothill oak
woodlands.

Peregrine falcons, rare in Yosemite, can dive at speeds of up
to 200 miles an hour (321 kph).

Male blue grouse inflates its neck sac to amplify "hooting"
sounds during elaborate courtship rituals.

White-tailed ptarmigan, a species successfully introduced
into the central High Sierra.

Mountain quail, easily identified by its two long, thin head
plumes, frequents chaparral and mountain meadows up to
8,000 feet (2438 m) in elevation.

Killdeer, rarely seen in the park, fakes a broken wing to lead intruders away from its nest.

ABOVE. Rare in Yosemite, a spotted owl perches in the
park's dense coniferous forests.
OPPOSITE. Distinguished by its ear tufts, the great horned owl
takes prey as large as porcupines, skunks, ducks, and grouse.

Noisy acorn woodpecker, common in Yosemite Valley,
stores acorns from California black oaks in holes drilled in
trees and other vertical surfaces.

Northern, or red-shafted, flicker guards its young.

Steller's jay, with its bright blue plumage and prominent crest, is a common and distinctive Yosemite bird.

Clark's nutcracker, frequently sighted in the High Sierra,
cracks and eats pine nuts and pilfers campsites.

A flash of indigo feathers marks the flight of the sparrow-sized western bluebird, which is fairly rare in the park.

Mountain bluebird at a nest cavity.

ABOVE. Yellow warbler feeding insects to its young.
OPPOSITE. Common yellowthroat (despite its name, quite
rare in the park) singing its loud, rolling *wichity
wichity wichity wich.*

Varied thrush, common in Yosemite's coniferous forests.

Bright yellow plumage and a bright orangish-red head make

Pine grosbeak, a plump bird found in the park's open
coniferous woods, uses a "gros" (French for large)
beak to crack nuts.

Cassin's finch is common in the park's open evergreen
woodlands and meadows up to 10,000 feet (3048 m).

Harmless California mountain kingsnake, one of 15 snake species in Yosemite, grows more than three feet (1 m) long.

Western terrestrial garter snake is a common resident of
meadows, ponds, and streams.

Suction pads on its toes enable the thumb-sized Pacific treefrog, the most abundant of Yosemite's eight kinds of frogs and toads, to climb vertical surfaces.

Bullfrog, North America's largest frog species, grows up to
eight inches (20 cm) in length.

Aʙᴏᴠᴇ. Cutthroat trout were introduced in high country lakes
from 1890 to 1914, when the U.S. Army managed the park.
Oᴘᴘᴏsɪᴛᴇ. Rainbow trout is the only native game fish
in Yosemite.

PLANTS

The park's tremendous range of elevations—from 2,000 feet (610 m) on the west to 13,000 feet (3,960 m) on the east—provides a wide variety of environments for trees, plants, and flowers. In fact, five of the seven continental life zones are found in Yosemite.

On the western edge of the park, up to elevations of about 3,500 feet (1,066 m), the oak-woodland belt mixes digger and ponderosa pine with black and canyon live oak. Meadows in these foothill woodlands are spiked in spring with blue and purple lupine, orange-gold California poppies, and other wildflowers, as well as the brilliant magenta blossoms of the western redbud shrub. South-facing hillsides are covered with dense brush, or chaparral, of manzanita, the hardest

Giant sequoias, Mariposa Grove, Wawona region.

wood in the Sierra Nevada.

A mixed-conifer forest extends from the oak-woodland belt to roughly 7,500 feet (2,286 m). The dominant species of Yosemite Valley are ramrod-straight ponderosa pines, which average 200 feet (60 m) in height and sport distinctive jigsaw-puzzle bark, and aromatic incense cedars, towering trees often mistaken for giant sequoias. Dogwoods thrive in the dense understory shade of California black oaks, producing a profusion of large, creamy white flowers in May and June.

Giant sequoias grow in moist pockets of this vegetation zone between 5,000 and 7,000 feet (1,524 m and 2,133 m). The trees reach their maximum height in about 800 years, then continue to add bulk for the next 2,000 years or so. Scientists believe that there are no built-in limits to the growth of the giant sequoias, which do not die of old age. Instead they succumb to high winds, heavy snows, and fire.

Yosemite's most complex and luxuriant forests thrive between 5,000 (1,524 m) and 8,500 feet (2,590 m), the elevation that receives maximum precipitation on the western slope of the Sierra Nevada. Wide areas of this zone are dominated by a lodgepole pine–red fir association.

A subalpine forest of lodgepole pine, whitebark pine, mountain hemlock, and western white pine begins at about 8,000 feet (2,438 m). Although at an elevation of 8,600 feet (2,621 m), Tuolumne Meadows is a luxuriant summer flower garden carpeted with elephant heads, cinquefoil, monkeyflower in various hues, larkspur, and Lemmon's paintbrush.

Forests dwindle to small groves at higher elevations. Trees peter out altogether at about 10,000 feet (3,048 m). Hardy wildflowers with tiny but intensely colored petals brighten the windswept heights—mountain sorrel, alpine saxifrage, rock primrose, ground-hugging mats of phlox, purple alpine penstemon, and Dana's lupine.

A field of harlequin and miniature lupine.

ABOVE. Whitebark pine, emblematic of the High Sierra,
grows all the way to the timberline.
OPPOSITE. White fir grows at high elevations, usually on
well-drained, north-facing slopes.

Lodgepole pine is the predominant tree in Yosemite's
subalpine forests.

Limber pines send roots deep into cracks in Yosemite
granite, then flex and bend in High Sierra winds.

ABOVE. Large, mealy seeds, or pine nuts, of the singleleaf pine are a favorite food of many birds and animals. OPPOSITE. The bark of the Jeffrey pine smells like vanilla or pineapple.

Ponderosa pine, the most common pine in North America.

Western white pine reaches heights of more than
100 feet (30 m).

ABOVE. Flat, yellow- or blue-green needles of the Douglas-fir grow on short or twisted leafstalks.

OPPOSITE. Massive bulk of giant sequoias, shown here in the Lower Grove of Mariposa, is supported by a web of feeder roots usually less than four feet (1.2 m) deep.

Above. Groves of quaking aspen grow in Yosemite Valley and in other sheltered locations.
Opposite. Western junipers, which can live up to 2,000 years, are easily identified by short, wide trunks and broad crowns of stout, spreading branches.

Black cottonwoods, the tallest native cottonwood, grow along Yosemite streams and rivers.

Canyon live oak, a common Yosemite tree on dry lower
mountain slopes and in canyons, has hollylike leaves.

Ahwahneechees made bows from the western redbud, a large, flowering shrub with showy pink petals.

White flowers of the red-osier dogwood appear in May at lower elevations and in valleys.

ABOVE. The aptly named bigleaf maple has the largest leaves
in the maple family: six to 10 inches (15 to 25 cm) across.
OPPOSITE. Pacific dogwood thrives in the dark understory of
coniferous forests, brightening somber dark-green
woodlands with early summer blossoms.

232

Yellow, starlike flowers of golden brodiaea, also known as pretty face, bloom from May to August.

Fern-leaved lomatium grows up to 5 feet (1.5 m) tall.

Ahwahneechees used the long, strong fibers of spreading
dogbane to make twine, nets, and clothing.

Each crownlike blossom of showy milkweed has five nectar
cups with smooth, incurved petals growing from them.

Flamboyant orange or yellow blooms of Sierra wallflower brighten Yosemite's oak-woodland belt.

Orange agoseris, or orange mountain dandelion, grows in
meadows and grassy openings in the park's coniferous forests.

ABOVE. Bull thistle's spiny stem ends in a rose-purple
powder-puff flower.
OPPOSITE. Wandering daisy, common in damp subalpine
and alpine meadows, is also known as the mountain daisy,
tall purple fleabane, and the mountain erigeron.

ABOVE. Golden yarrow, which thrives in Yosemite's oak-woodland belt, contains a chemical that speeds blood clotting. OPPOSITE. Heads of common madia, a member of the sunflower family, close at night.

Greenleaf raillardella, an alpine sunflower that blooms in July and August, grows on dry rocky ridges and in gravelly areas.

Black-eyed Susan, Maryland's state flower, spread across
the continent as a garden flower and now grows wild in
Yosemite's meadows and open woods at lower elevations.

245

ABOVE. Pinwheels of bright red petals distinguish the Indian pink, one of the showiest western wildflowers.
OPPOSITE. Arrowhead groundsel often grows in large clumps along streams and in subalpine meadows.

Canyon dudleya, or live-forever, grows along arid, rocky
cliffs and dry, open woodlands.

Succulent stems and leaves of the Sierra sedum, also called
the stonecrop, store water to ensure the plant's survival
during drought.

Red-tipped sepals add a blush of color to the snowy,
bell-like flowers of white heather, John Muir's
favorite alpine flower.

Alpine laurel's deep pink flowers bloom in High Sierra bogs
and wet meadows from June through September.

Above. Dense clumps of mountain heather form extensive mats on open rocky slopes.

Opposite. Bush lupines, which flower from April to June with deep blue blossoms, are found at lower elevations in Yosemite, especially from El Portal to Yosemite Valley.

Miniature lupine, found in grassy meadows at low elevations.

Brewer's lupine, a matting variety that seldom grows more than six inches (15 cm) tall, blooms along Tioga Road and Glacier Point Road from June to August.

Whiteworl lupines break out in dense clusters of white and occasionally pink flowers on grassy hillsides at lower elevations from April to June.

Harlequin lupine, distinguished by tri-colored "pea flowers"
of yellow, white, and rose.

ABOVE. Western bleeding heart, which grows in dense woods, gets its name from the pinkish-purple, heart-shaped flowers that dangle from the stem.
OPPOSITE. A favorite springtime wildflower, baby blue eyes grow in moist valleys and on hillsides in oak woodlands and chaparral.

ABOVE. Blue-eyed grasses are identified as members of the iris family by the way their narrow, sword-shaped leaves overlap near the base and by the three stamens in the center of each flower.
OPPOSITE. Petals of the Rocky Mountain iris range in color from blue to lilac.

ABOVE. Delicate blue flowers of the western blue flax bloom from slender stalks nearly three feet (1 m) high. OPPOSITE. Fragrant, trumpetlike white flowers of the Washington lily are often mottled with purple dots.

ABOVE. Primarily a desert plant, the giant blazing star also grows on arid, south-facing slopes in Yosemite foothills. **OPPOSITE.** Yellow water lily's bright waxy flowers, which grow up to four inches (10 cm) across, brighten the dark waters of Yosemite's High Sierra ponds.

Dudley's clarkia, a member of the evening primrose family.

Fireweed carpets burned or logged forest floors with their
pink spires.

Spotted coralroot has a wandlike cluster of purplish flowers atop a leafless stalk.

Mountain lady's slipper, an orchid of open or lightly shaded valleys and slopes.

Bog rein orchid grows fragrant white flowers.

Hooded ladies' tresses are found in moist meadows and
forest clearings.

ABOVE. Huge, aromatic flowers of matilija poppy blossom in Yosemite's dry oak woodlands.
OPPOSITE. A field of nodding California poppies, the Golden State's official flower.

ABOVE. Broad, flat flowers of mountain phlox, or spreading phlox, range in color from white to pale lilac.
OPPOSITE. Showy pink flowers of mustang clover, or mustang linanthus, with their distinctive yellow throats, bloom from May to July in open woodlands and dry gravelly slopes at low elevations.

Pussy paws, named for fuzzy clusters of densely packed
flowers that look like the upturned pads of a cat's foot.

Snow plant, a stout, fleshy, startlingly bright red member of
the wintergreen family.

ABOVE. Each of the five petals of the red columbine stretches back into a distinctive, nectar-rich spur that attracts pollinating insects.

OPPOSITE. Shrubby cinquefoil flowers from June to August in open forests and meadows throughout the park.

Wild rose, or woods rose, a widely distributed flowering shrub.

Thimbleberry's Latin name, *parviflorus*, or "small-flowered," refers to this shrub's two-inch-wide (5-cm) white flowers.

Above. Rose-pink flowers of mountain spiraea, or pink meadowsweet, sweetly scent wet meadows and other boggy areas near the Yosemite timberline.

Opposite. Spring brings a bouquet of small white flowers to the Lewis' syringa, or mock orange.

Variable hues of Indian paintbrush—blood-red, delicate
pink, orange, yellow, and white—come not from the plant's
drab tubular flowers but from the colorful floral bracts
which enfold them.

Drooping, thimble-shaped flowers of foxglove.

Lewis' monkeyflower attracts hummingbirds during High
Sierra summers.

Elephant head, named for flowers shaped like elephants'
heads with upraised trunks.

ABOVE. Cascade penstemon raises deep blue to dark purple flowers from June to August atop a tall, serrated stem that gives the plant its Latin name, *serrulatus.*
OPPOSITE. Davidson's penstemon crowds blue-lavender flowers on a base of matted stems.

Blue penstemon blossoms in open, sunny locations atop a
sticky, hairy stem up to 24 inches (61 cm) tall.

Mountain pride, a penstemon that spreads pink swards
from June to August across the High Sierra.

TRAVEL TIPS

More than 4 million people come here each year; three-quarters of them head for Yosemite Valley, which covers about 1 percent of the park's 1,200 square miles (3,100 sq km). Expect filled campgrounds and roofed accommodations in the valley from June through August and some crowding in late spring and early autumn. Reservations are essential for overnight visits.

The park is open year-round. Summer weather is warm and dry, with temperatures reaching 100° F (37.7° C) in Yosemite Valley and 75° F (23.8° C) in the High Sierra; nights are always cool. Winter temperatures range from 15° F (-9.4° C) to 40° F (4.4° C), with abundant sunshine. Snow starts to fall in mid-November, closing Tioga Road until as late as mid-June.

There are five entrances, three on the west, one on the south, and one on the east. The Hetch Hetchy Entrance is the northernmost western entrance. The Arch Rock Entrance is about eighty-one miles (130 km) west of Merced via Highway 140. The Big Oak Flat Entrance is accessible via Highway 120.

From the south, take Highway 41 ninety-four miles (151 km) north from Fresno to the South Entrance. From the east follow Highway 120 from the town of Lee Vining to the Tioga Pass Entrance, which is open in the summer only.

Bus, rail, and air service is available to Merced and Fresno, with connecting bus service to the park. Reno–Lake Tahoe airports offer the closest access to the Tioga Pass Entrance.

Visiting Yosemite National Park

Address   Yosemite National Park
P.O. Box 577
California 95389
(209) 372-0264

Visitor Centers

The Valley Visitor Center in Yosemite Village dispenses information, maps, and publications. A short slide show introduces the park's natural and human history. The Indian Cultural Exhibit next door displays baskets, tools, and other Miwok artifacts. In summer inter-

293

preters demonstrate basket weaving, food preparation, and other arts and crafts in the re-created Miwok village. The walls of the Fine Arts Gallery adjacent to the cultural exhibit are hung with artistic interpretations of Yosemite's grandeur.

At the eastern end of the valley the Happy Isles Nature Center, open summer and early fall, also distributes interpretive material. The center's Junior Ranger Program for children is the oldest in America.

The Mariposa Grove Museum, open from mid-May to mid-October, contains exhibits that explain the life history of the giant sequoia. The Pioneer Yosemite History Center at Wawona consists of furnished historic buildings moved here from their original settings. Costumed guides portray people and activities from the park's storied past. On the grounds of the nearby Wawona Hotel is Thomas Hill's studio, where reproductions of the artist's works are displayed in summer.

Tuolumne Meadows Visitor Center, open only in summer, contains fascinating exhibits on subalpine and alpine ecology; the pressed wildflower collection is lovely. Displays at Parsons Lodge, built in 1915 near Soda Springs, concentrate on the human history of the meadows. The lodge is a one-mile (1.6-km) walk from the Lembert Dome parking lot.

Park Fees

A $5 entrance fee for private, noncommercial vehicles includes multiple entries.

Facilities for the Disabled

Visitor centers, the nature and art centers, and some trails are wheelchair accessible. A free brochure itemizing facilities for the disabled is available from visitor centers and by writing Park Headquarters.

Accommodations

The park's roofed facilities are operated by the Yosemite Park and Curry Co., 5410 East Home Ave., Fresno, California 93727. Call (209) 252-4848 for reservations at the Wawona Hotel (105 rooms, pool, restaurant, spring through October); Yosemite Lodge (306 rooms, 189 cabins, pool, restaurant); Ahwahnee Hotel (123 units, pool, restaurant); Curry Village (18 rooms, 183 cabins, 427 tent-cabins, pool, restaurant); White Wolf Lodge (4 cabins, 24 tent-cabins, restaurant, summer only); and Tuolumne Meadows Lodge (69 tent-cabins, summer only). Tuolumne Meadows Lodge is the only one of the five High Sierra tent-camps that is accessible by car. The other five tent-camps (meals, summer only, reserve by mail from early December) are in the back-country.

Campgrounds

There are fifteen campgrounds in addition to the High Sierra camps. Summer stays are limited to two to fourteen days; a thirty-day limit is in effect the rest of the year. For information, call (209) 372-0200. For reservations, call any Ticketron outlet or write Ticketron Parks Department, Pembroke 5, Suite 423, Virginia Beach, Virginia 23462. Reservations are required year-round for campgrounds in Yosemite Valley and at the Hodgdon Meadow Campground near the Big Oak Flat Entrance. Reservations are required for the Crane Flat Campground from spring through fall, and for half of the Tuolumne Meadows campsites in summer. Other campgrounds are first come, first served. In summer most fill by 2:00 P.M.

Free permits are required for overnight backpack trips. Except from February 1 to May 31, permits are issued first come, first served. You can apply at the Wilderness Permit Station up to twenty-four hours in advance of a trip. Between the above dates, half of the permits are available through the mail.

Outdoor Activities
Short Itineraries

Driving around Yosemite and visiting just some of the major attractions would take a minimum of two full days. Expect to average about thirty miles (50 km) an hour on congested park highways.

For first-time visitors with only one day, drive through Yosemite Valley early in the morning, stopping at various scenic turnouts. Also drop by the visitor center for an overview of the park and be sure to walk to the base of Yosemite Fall. Depending on traffic and how long you linger in the valley, you'll probably have time to drive to Glacier Point or tour the giant sequoias at Mariposa.

A weekend excursion might include the above itinerary for the first day, then a second day's drive into the High Sierra on Tioga Road. Be sure to turn around before you exit the park; there can be hour-long waits to re-enter Yosemite from the east.

A long weekend itinerary might include the above, as well as time for nature walks (try trails to Taft Point, Sentinel Dome, and Vernal Fall, and at Tuolumne Meadows).

Wildlife Viewing

The park protects habitats for 80 species of mammals and 247 kinds of birds. Following are prime viewing areas.

Wawona Region

The meadows, oak woodlands, chaparral, and sequoia forest of the Wawona Basin, dissected by the South Fork of the Merced River, are home to more than a hundred kinds of birds. American robins and Steller's jays are most common. Mule deer are often seen browsing in Wawona Meadows and at Mariposa's Upper Grove.

Yosemite Valley Region

This is the other most likely locale for sighting mule deer, especially at dawn or dusk in Cook's Meadow, south of the Valley Visitor Center. Scrounging black bears are frequent and unwelcome visitors to valley campgrounds. Coyotes are elusive during the three warm seasons, but in winter they boldly prowl the valley floor. Ducks and geese overwinter along the Merced, which never totally freezes over.

Tuolumne Meadows

The most common mammals are Belding ground squirrels, gregarious denizens of meadows, and yellow-bellied marmots, inhabitants of rock piles. California bighorn sheep are occasionally sighted hereabouts. About twenty kinds of birds are common residents of Tuolumne, including the dark-eyed junco, blue grouse, and Clark's nutcracker.

High Sierra

Life is demanding in the subalpine and alpine regions. Mammals adapt to short summers and long, harsh winters by storing food (pikas) or building up body fat for hibernation (marmots). Birds, the most common vertebrates, increase their chances of survival by winging between several life zones for food.

Hiking

Trails totaling 800 miles (1,287 km) lead hikers along valley floors and rugged backcountry.

Short walks suitable for all ages are scattered throughout the park. In the Mariposa Grove, trails gently ascend 1,000 feet (300 m) over 2.5 miles (4 km) from the Lower Grove to the peaceful Upper Grove. A half-hour side trip from the Galen Clark Tree in the Upper Grove heads north to views of the Wawona Basin from Wawona Point. Some visitors may prefer to take one of the open-air trams to the Upper Grove and stroll downhill back to the parking lot.

Two scenic walks begin at the same parking lot along the Glacier Point Road, about six miles (9.6 km) past Bridalveil Campground. The Sentinel Dome Trail heads 1.1 mile (1.8 km) northeast to a bald granite dome pocked with eroded basins and crowned with the gnarled limbs of a dead Jeffrey pine as bleached as driftwood. One thousand feet (300 m) higher than Glacier Point, Sentinel Dome presents unobscured 360-degree views. Time your hike to coincide with a full moon or as the setting sun spreads its roseate glow over Yosemite.

The Taft Point Trail heads the same distance west from the parking lot to an overhanging lookout on the rim of the valley with great views of the Cathedral Rocks and Spires and the north rim. En route are the Fissures, extraordinarily deep, narrow clefts in the granite.

In the Yosemite Valley a broad, paved trail goes .25 miles (.4 km) from the Lower Yosemite Fall parking lot to the base of the cataract. For a closer look at Upper Yosemite Fall, hike the first half of a strenuous, 3.6-mile (5.8-km) switchback trail from Sunnyside

Campground. Stop at Columbia Rock, one mile (1.6 km) up the trail, for valley views.

The Mirror Lake Trail makes a pleasant, if horse-rutted, three-mile (4.8-km) loop that takes in this tiny lake and both banks of Tenaya Creek. The moderately strenuous (and usually congested) 1.5-mile (2.4-km) Mist Trail begins at the Happy Isles Nature Center, crosses Vernal Fall Bridge, where there are excellent views of the cataract, then switchbacks up a rock stairway of more than 500 steps to the brink of the fall. About three miles (4.8 km) from the start of the Big Oak Flat Road, the Big Oak Flat Trail winds one mile (1.6 km) north through a recent burn that blooms with lupines and other wildflowers in June.

In the Tioga Road touring region, a ten-minute walk at Olmsted Point crosses rock scraped clean by glaciers. Dwarf trees and erratics are also passed, and marmots are often seen here.

A roughly circular, moderately difficult fifty-mile (80-km) trail links the five backcountry High Sierra camps and Tuolumne Meadows Lodge on Tioga Road. The camps, spaced about a day's hike apart, make it possible to trek alpine wilderness encumbered only by a day pack. The route is so popular that trailhead quotas are used to limit the number of hikers. Make reservations in early January for summer treks.

At Tuolumne Meadows, a hundred-yard (90-m) trail from a picnic area just east of the visitor center on Tioga Road leads to the lower slopes of Lembert Dome. Most visitors prefer this easy walk with its sweeping views to the more rigorous route that circles around the backside of the dome and ascends to its summit.

Cycling

This is a popular way to sightsee in Yosemite Valley. Eight miles (12.8 km) of valley bikeway are separated from automobile traffic. Rentals by the hour or the day are available at the Yosemite Lodge Bike Stand and the Curry Village Bike Stand. The Chilnualna Falls Road and Forest Drive at Wawona are also popular.

Swimming

Beaches and swimming holes line the South Fork of the Merced River in the Wawona Meadows. Beaches also line stretches of the Merced River, chilly even in mid-summer. Mirror Lake is also popular for valley swims. In the backcountry, the beach at the eastern end of Tenaya Lake beckons water lovers, as do several forks of the Tuolumne River at Tuolumne Meadows.

Fishing

Only rainbow trout are indigenous to park waters. Systematic stocking, which began in 1892, has left self-sustaining trout populations in more than 100 of Yosemite's 318 major lakes. Thirteen park lakes are still stocked on a limited basis. Trout species include rainbow, eastern brook, brown, golden, and cutthroat. Favorite fishing holes include high-country lakes (Lukens, Harden, Tenaya, May, Dog, Cathedral, and Elizabeth), Yosemite Creek, and the Dana Fork of the Tuolumne River. Various limits and restrictions apply. Fishing permits are required.

Boating

Motorless craft may be used on these lakes: Tenaya, Merced, May, Benson, Tilden, Twin, Kibbie, and Many Island. Hetch Hetchy Reservoir is off-limits. Kayaks and canoes may be used on the Merced without a permit.

Rafting

A concession at Curry Village sends flotillas of rafters down the Merced River in summer.

Horseback Riding

Stables are located at Wawona, White Wolf, Tuolumne Meadows, and Yosemite Valley.

Climbing

Yosemite Valley offers the most difficult rock climbing in the contiguous United States; El Capitan's 3,500-foot (1,066-m) vertical walls offer one of the great rock-climbing challenges in the world.

Other popular climbing areas include relatively uncrowded Tuolumne Meadows, where most climbs are on glacier-polished domes (Lembert, Pywiack) and the slabs north of Tioga Road at Tenaya Lake, as well as other sites farther east at the Sierran crest.

Winter Activities

At Crane Flat, cold-weather recreation includes cross-country skiing and ranger-led snowshoe walks and ski tours. Rangers also lead walks through Mariposa Grove.

The Badger Pass Ski Area on Glacier Point Road, California's oldest ski resort (1935), has ten modest downhill runs. Cross-country trails include one route that goes all the way to Glacier Point, where Yosemite Concession Services operates a winter hut; call (209) 372-8444 for information. Another favorite cross-country route is to 9,500-foot (2,895-m) Horse Ridge. Contact the Yosemite Association by writing P.O. Box 545, Yosemite National Park, California 95389, or by calling (209) 372-0740 to reserve the Ostrander Lake Ski Hut, just below the north face of the ridge.

There is ice skating on the outdoor rink at Curry Village.

Wildlife Viewing

Location Key

WB Wawona Basin

YV Yosemite Valley

TM Tuolumne Meadows

HS High Sierra

WF Western Foothills

Mammals

- ☐ Black bear YV, TM, HS, WF, WB
- ☐ Badger WB, YV, TM, WF
- ☐ California bighorn sheep HS
- ☐ Bobcat WB, YV, WF
- ☐ Chickaree WB, YV, TM, HS
- ☐ Chipmunk TM, HS
- ☐ Coyote WB, YV, TM, HS, TM, WF
- ☐ Mule deer WB, YV, TM, HS, WF
- ☐ Ermine TM, HS
- ☐ Gray fox WB, YV, WF
- ☐ Ground squirrel, Belding TM, HS
- ☐ Ground squirrel, California WB, YV, WF
- ☐ Ground squirrel, Golden-mantled TM, HS
- ☐ Mountain lion WB, YV, TM, HS, WF
- ☐ Yellow-bellied marmot TM, HS
- ☐ Mink TM, HS
- ☐ Deer mouse WB, YV, TM, HS, WF
- ☐ River otter YV, TM
- ☐ Pika TM, HS
- ☐ Ringtail raccoon WB, YV, WF
- ☐ Western gray squirrel WB, YV

Birds

- ☐ Brewer's blackbird WB, YV, WF
- ☐ Mountain bluebird HS, TM
- ☐ Mountain chickadee WB, HS, WF, YV, TM
- ☐ American dipper WB, HS, YV, TM, WF
- ☐ Golden eagle HS, WF, WB, YV, TM
- ☐ Finch, Gray-crowned rosy HS, TM
- ☐ Finch, Cassins YV, TM
- ☐ Black-headed grosbeak WB, YV, WF

- ☐ Blue grouse **WB, TM**
- ☐ Red-tailed hawk **WB, YV, TM, HS, WF**
- ☐ Steller's jay **WB, YV, TM**
- ☐ Belted kingfisher **WB, YV, TM, WF**
- ☐ Clark's nutcracker **TM, HS**
- ☐ Red-breasted nuthatch **HS, YV, WB, TM**
- ☐ Great-horned owl **WB, YV, WF, TM**
- ☐ Mountain quail **WB, YV**
- ☐ Band-tailed pigeon **YV**
- ☐ American robin **YV, WB, WF, TM**
- ☐ Warbler, black-throated gray **WB, WF, YV**
- ☐ Warbler, yellow **WB, YV, WF**
- ☐ Acorn woodpecker **WB, YV, WF**

PARK CONSERVATION

The first national parks were created out of a sense of cultural identity, as a way to take pride in something uniquely American. Since then, citizens have played an active role in park protection, speaking out on behalf of sound park management; monitoring inappropriate use of parklands; identifying adjacent land activities threatening park resources; and publicizing those issues to park personnel, the media, and the public. Local action has always been critical to park protection. Here are some basic ways to take action at your park and to understand its needs.

How much time can you spare?

A Few Hours a Month

Read and Research

Park-related issues and stories are at the forefront of the environmental movement. Activists must first educate themselves on park issues before they can begin the process of educating others.

Join a local or national park advocacy organization

Park groups rely on active membership bases to support programs, fund educational materials, and to increase the visibility of park issues among the media, elected officials, the Park Service, and the general public. Most groups provide their members with newsletters or magazines that are good primers for understanding specific park issues and give suggestions of action to take in response. Local park advocacy groups have smaller memberships and fewer resources than their counterparts at the national level. National park advocacy groups involve their members in special activist corps by recruiting them to work on key park issues at the local level.

Write letters and make phone calls

Raise the level of awareness of your elected officials and park issues by writing or phoning them

for their position. This will let them know that
their constituents care about the problems fac-
ing national parks and are interested in how government works to solve these problems. An
informed constituency creates a heightened
response to park problems.

One Day a Month

Attend the meeting of your local park group

These meetings provide an important way to
meet with other park activists. It's also a good
way to let others know you want to do something
for your park.

Get on the park mailing list

Parks maintain mailing lists of citizens who want
to be informed of any management actions. Ask
to be placed on the list for your parks and stress
that you want to be notified of any opportunities
to participate in "scoping." (Scoping is an agen-
cy's solicitation of public opinion on an action.)

Go visit your park

Become familiar with your park so that you are
able to notice when the park is being improved,
neglected, or altered in any way. When you do

notice a problem, be sure to alert the park. Either write to the superintendent and ask for a response, or call and ask for the person who handles the type of problem you are reporting. Also alert your local and national advocacy groups.

Write a letter to the editor for your local newspaper
> The news media are important in raising the visibility of park issues.

A Few Days a Month or More

Volunteer
> To do volunteer work, contact your park directly or contact the National Park Service interpretation division at (202) 619-7077 and ask for information on becoming a volunteer.

Develop relationships with the park staff
> Become familiar with your park's staff and their duties.

Participate in park planning
> National Park Service (NPS) policies require public involvement. The general management plan is the comprehensive plan for your park and should be guiding decisions made by NPS staff. Become familiar with this document so that you

311

have a point of reference for any activity occurring in the park. Make sure you are on the park mailing list. Activists should offer comments on all park management plans.

Build a network of people in your community interested in protecting your park

If there is a park advocacy group in your area, be an active member and help recruit interested local community members (contact NPCA for a park advocacy group in your area). Seek to develop a well-rounded coalition that represents all aspects of the community.

Your involvement in protecting national parks becomes more important every day. As development pressures make open space increasingly scarce, ecosystems and wildlife habitat that depend on parks and their adjacent lands are being destroyed at a growing rate. America's cultural heritage is being paved over to build suburban shopping malls. Park budgets are being cut at an even faster rate. The battle to protect our national parks is a continuing challenge. A committed, vocal community of park supporters is key to winning the battle.

The National Parks and Conservation Association (NPCA) is America's only private nonprofit citizen organization dedicated solely to protecting, preserving, and enhancing the U.S. National Park System. Founded in 1919 as an association of "Citizens Protecting America's Parks," NPCA has more than 450,000 members.

To become a member of NPCA, send a tax-deductible membership contribution of $25 to: NPCA, 1776 Massachusetts Avenue, N.W., Washington, D.C. 20036. Members receive *National Parks,* an award-winning bimonthly magazine.

INDEX

I'd like to thank Continental Airlines for its generous assistance
—DAVID DUNBAR

All photographs are by Jerry Pavia except the following: © Sonja Bullaty, NY: 154–65, 178; © John D. Cunningham/Visuals Unlimited, NH: 153, 190; © Derrick Ditchburn/Visuals Unlimited, NH: 202; © Don W. Fawcett/Visuals Unlimited, NH: 192; © Dede Gilman/Unicorn Stock Photos, MO: 206; © Stephen J. Lang/Visuals Unlimited, NH: 201; © Tom and Pat Leeson, WA: 148, 152, 158–61, 163–64, 168, 171–73, 180–84, 186–89, 191, 193, 195–96, 199, 208, 210; © Jane McAlonan/Visuals Unlimited, NH: 198; Joe McDonald/Visuals Unlimited, NH: 207, 209; S. Maslowski/Visuals Unlimited, NH: 170, 204; © Michael S. Quinton, AK: 150, 157, 162, 164, 167, 169, 174–77, 185, 197, 205, 211; © Tom J. Ulrich/Visuals Unlimited, NH: 194, 200 203; © W.J. Weber/Visuals Unlimited, NH: 166.

SELECTED TINY FOLIOS™
AVAILABLE FROM ABBEVILLE PRESS

- Ansel Adams: The National Park Service Photographs
  1-55859-817-0 ▪ $11.95
- Audubon's Birds of America:
  The Audubon Society Baby Elephant Folio
  1-55859-225-3 ▪ $11.95
- Everglades National Park
  1-55859-827-8 ▪ $11.95
- The Great Book of Currier & Ives' America
  1-55859-229-6 ▪ $11.95
- The Great Book of French Impressionism
  1-55859-336-5 ▪ $11.95
- Minerals and Gems from the American Museum
  of Natural History
  1-55859-273-3 ▪ $11.95
- Norman Rockwell: 332 Magazine Covers
  1-55859-224-5 ▪ $11.95
- The North American Indian Portfolios:
  Bodmer, Catlin, McKenney & Hall
  1-55859-601-1 ▪ $11.95
- Treasures of Disney Animation Art
  1-55859-335-7 ▪ $11.95
- Treasures of Folk Art: The Museum of American Folk Art
  1-55859-560-0 ▪ $11.95
- Wild Flowers of America
  1-55859-564-3 ▪ $11.95
- Yellowstone National Park
  1-55859-825-1 ▪ $11.95